Natural Disasters

Wildfires

by Julie Murray

3

Dash!
LEVELED READERS
An Imprint of Abdo Zoom • abdobooks.com

Dash!
LEVELED READERS

Level 1 – Beginning
Short and simple sentences with familiar words or patterns for children who are beginning to understand how letters and sounds go together.

Level 2 – Emerging
Longer words and sentences with more complex language patterns for readers who are practicing common words and letter sounds.

Level 3 – Transitional
More developed language and vocabulary for readers who are becoming more independent.

THIS BOOK CONTAINS RECYCLED MATERIALS

abdobooks.com

Published by Abdo Zoom, a division of ABDO, PO Box 398166, Minneapolis, Minnesota 55439.

Printed in the United States of America, North Mankato, Minnesota.
052024
092024

Photo Credits: Shutterstock
Production Contributors: Kenny Abdo, Jennie Forsberg, Grace Hansen, John Hansen
Design Contributors: Candice Keimig, Neil Klinepier

Library of Congress Control Number: 2023948529

Publisher's Cataloging in Publication Data

Names: Murray, Julie, author.
Title: Wildfires / by Julie Murray
Description: Minneapolis, Minnesota : Abdo Zoom, 2025 | Series: Natural disasters | Includes online resources and index.
Identifiers: ISBN 9781098285548 (lib. bdg.) | ISBN 9781098286248 (ebook) | ISBN 9781098286590 (Read-to-me eBook)
Subjects: LCSH: Natural disasters--Juvenile literature. | Wildfires--Juvenile literature. | Bush fires-Juvenile literature. | Climate and wildfires--Juvenile literature.
Classification: DDC 904.5--dc23

Table of Contents

Wildfires

Wildfires are uncontrolled fires. They begin in forests, grasslands, or other wild areas. Sometimes they burn where people and animals live too. Wildfires can quickly become a natural disaster!

Wildfires can be caused by a natural event such as a lightning strike. But most wildfires are started by careless human acts, such as leaving a bonfire unattended or throwing out a lit cigarette.

The Fire Triangle

Fires need three things to exist: heat, **fuel**, and oxygen. These things make up what is known as the "Fire Triangle."

Oxygen is a gas in the air that we breathe. A fire needs oxygen to burn. Cutting off the fire's oxygen source is a way to put it out.

Fuel is also needed. Leaves, grass, trees, and shrubs are all fuel sources for a fire.

Dry conditions, such as a **drought**, make the fuel easier to catch on fire.

Lastly, fires need a heat source. The heat source starts the fire. Lightning, the sun, or a human act can all provide a heat source. Once **ignited**, the fire feeds on **fuel** around it. It is **sustained** by oxygen in the air.

Effects

Wildfires can be devastating! They can burn everything in their paths. They can move quickly and are **unpredictable**. Wildfires can travel up to 14 miles per hour (22.5 kph)!

Smoke from a wildfire fills the air and can stretch for hundreds of miles. Falling ash can cover homes. Blowing **embers** can spark new fires.

Firefighters work hard to put out wildfires. Planes can be used to drop water or chemicals on a fire. This helps stop the fire from spreading.

Firefighters also help evacuate people. They save lives!

More Facts

- The temperature inside a wildfire can reach more than 2,000 degrees F (1,093 degrees C).
- Wildfires can produce a firestorm. This is when a fire is so intense that it creates its own weather pattern. It can produce winds up to 70 miles per hour (112 kph).
- Wildfires travel uphill quicker than downhill. This is mainly because heat rises.

Glossary

drought – a long period with little or no rain.

ember – a small piece of glowing wood from a fire.

fuel – a source of energy.

ignited – caused to begin burning or to set on fire.

sustained – maintained for a long time without weakening.

unpredictable – not able to be known beforehand.

Index

Online Resources

Booklinks
NONFICTION NETWORK
FREE! ONLINE NONFICTION RESOURCES

To learn more about Wildfires, please visit **abdobooklinks.com** or scan this QR code. These links are routinely monitored and updated to provide the most current information available.